Thawed Stars

Thawed Stars

Poems

by Alice Pero

For Amy ~
Please enjoy my
book.
Happy Spring!
Best wishes —
Alice Pero
March
2024

SunInk Publications, Carmel, California

These poems were first published in the following publications:

"Thawed Stars" Co-op City Times
"This Isn't Enough" Co-op City Times
"Down the Balustrade" Co-op City Times
"Periods of Rain" Co-op City Times
"The Curtains" Co-op City Times
"Debauch" Words and Pictures
"Lightning and the Moon" Words and Pictures
"The Apples" Three Mile Harbor and The California Poetry Calendar
"Remembrance" Three Mile Harbor
"Conversation" Salonika
"Edges I" Salonika
"My Mother" Salonika and Poetry Now
"Rain Moments on the Train" Salonika and The California Poetry Calendar
"Night Sky" Poetry Now
"Edges II" Poetry Now
"Voyage Out of Old Skin" The Second Word Thursdays Anthology

The author would like to thank Russell Salamon for invaluable assistance in the making of this book.

Cover painting, illustrations by Bruce Silton.

Back cover photo by Mary Wright.

(paperback) 9 8 7 6 5 4 3 2 1

THAWED STARS

Library of Congress Catalogue Card No. 99-093761

ISBN 0-931104-47-5

For Sky, Arwen, Amy and Erik

Introduction

Alice Pero, whose name echoes Alice in Wonderland, is a wonderland speaking, but not only speaking. This is flight talk of butterflies in rebellion with natural laws. This is a woman who loves men and trees and beings and turtles and trains screeching around a curve through the rain.

In simple words the air between trees stands naked with birch trees and in another turn of page you feast on a roast rack of angel meat. Is nothing sacred? Only the poet. Only the listener. Universes are not sacred but are to be eaten like oranges with strange chambers, houses on hills.

Young boys run bringing the wind, leap out of their bodies for a swim, seven days in blue sky and seven nights in the arms of a sofa with tea and cookies and excited eyes strong with future worlds.

You may feel raindrops dripping from your hair as you read these lines. You may feel your breath rushing away to play among smoking mountains, mist over the hills echoing with howls of coyotes.

These poems may be unhuman, and to read them, you may have to become divine light among houses covered with snow.

Russell Salamon

Table of Contents

CHAPTER THREE, THE EVIDENCE

CHAPTER FOUR, LOST/FOUND

CHAPTER FIVE, THESE BIRCHES/THIS SUN

Thawed Stars

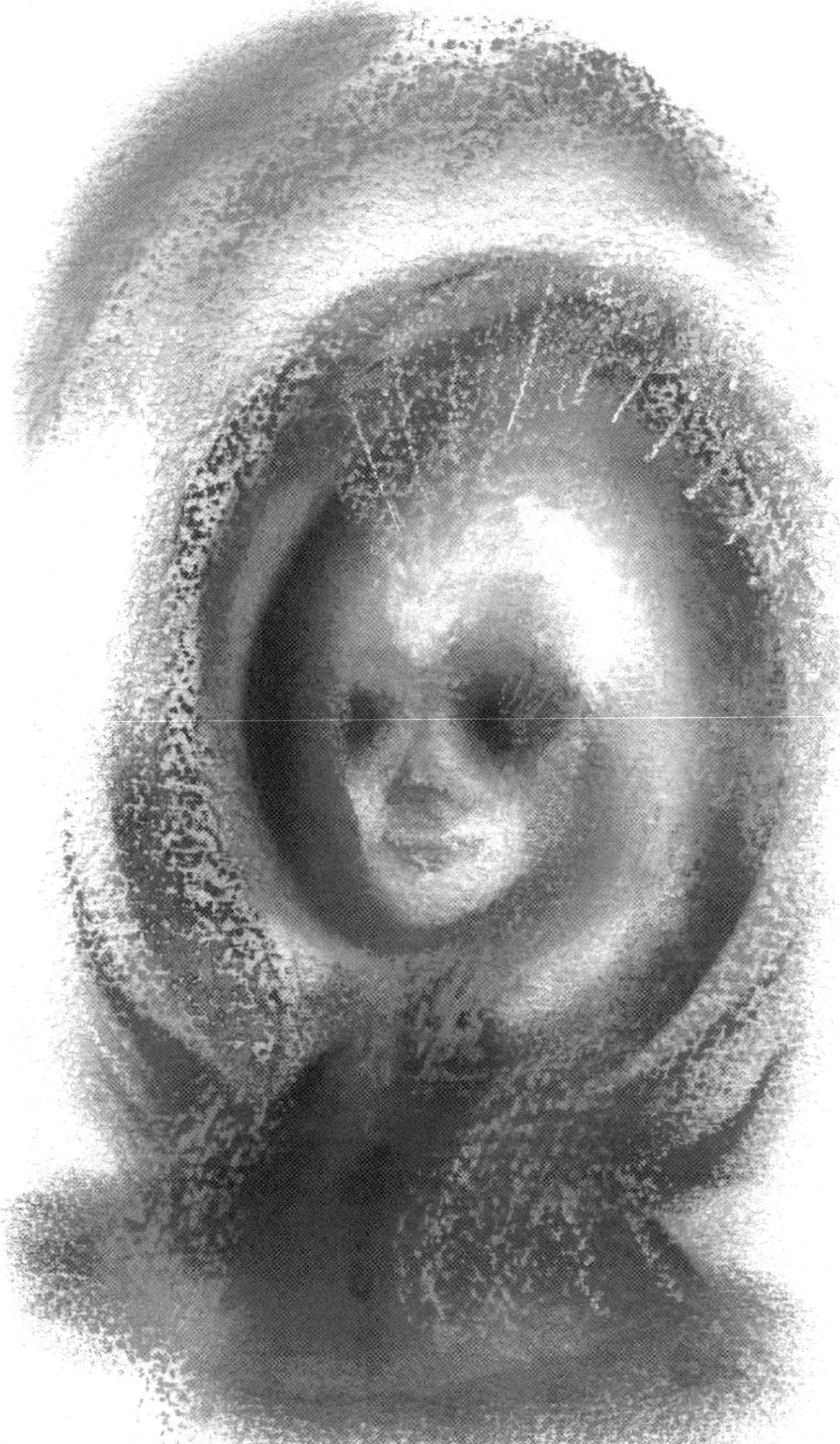

Chapter One

New Music

TRAVEL

Portions of this poem
have been read before
at breakfast in another year
before the winds of space
took my love away
and blew me to machines and time.
Portions of this poem,
not seen by traveling eyes,
were found again in new-lit trees
by voyagers who knew the way
to unmaking moments.
Why travel far? say I,
when poems speak here
in our instant universe.

NIGHT SKY

Last night I stole the night sky
I wanted a long long black cloak
to sleep in
I was restless
and couldn't settle down
You are probably wondering
what I did with the myriad of stars
I wasn't intending to dazzle
I only wanted to lie down
with the comfortable weight
of the dark night sky
wrap myself in its deep dream,
the silent splendor of darkness
If anyone missed it, I do not know
This morning I released the sky,
tied it to its moorings—the stars—
Saw it turn blue again in sun
none the worse for the wear.

TO SING AWAY THE MICE IN YOUR CUPBOARDS

Sing roar and syncopate
The sycophants yawn and scurry
Ding dong ring go free
The listless men arise and fling
their dead thoughts to the breeze
Your soft laugh permeates
You fly far aloft
above the mendicants
the wheezing of humanity, lamenting
You blow with the birds
The living dead crack down to bones in
earth
and the mice in your cupboards
run off.

GREEN-PURPLE MARSHMALLOW MONSTER

Green-purple marshmallow monster
Words pour out in odd cascades
from your unearthly mouth
I see you in a cloud parallel
to this man-tired universe.
Sea porpoise soprano,
singing all the wishing fish notes
higher than my woman-ears can hear
You rest in an ecstasy flash
under all the rainbows
Pot of gold does not shine
but undulates a golden glow
Why are my eyes so slow?
They drift away and only see
that neon sign.

THE SMALL SHOP

How many times have you longed
to open up a small shop
and sell your wares?
Honeyed pancakes
Rare smiling eyes
Religious tokens, bits of ecstasy
Famous person's ties
And the times you'll always remember
The kiss in the rowboat
The wig you wished you hadn't worn once
And the race through raindrops
when, miraculously, you didn't get wet
That brings us back to miracles
Oh small shop, I take you and fold you up
And put you on the permanent street
of my dreams

I COULD WRITE UNTIL THE NIGHT...

I could write until the night
caves into day
and back again
The rose drops off, bud appears
once more
The roar of ocean turns to drip
and drip to roar
I cannot be lost
Upheavals, bloody battles,
shore to shore
I will find my words, my thoughts
not shelved, not dust
I need nothing, I am loose, trimmed
of fat
The fat of time won't stick
to my cell-less self
I will right myself from each tumble
and I will fall in with me next time
each time, again

FRIEND

I knew you before the moon was lit
the learned men
were beardless and bodiless
and apples grew on the wingtips
of flying trees
I was your friend in light
The light that went faster than
any measurement
And souls were the source
of every merriment
I knew you before the ruin that hit
when there weren't any dens of fear,
inhabitants who babbled lies
And only songs were real

INSPIRATION

I can't believe it!
she cried.
Sparkles from her eyes
Renewed six gardens,
Flashed unearthly passions
to ten thousand supine minds.
Such a violent inspiration,
silently dispersed,
Sixty cows gave extra bellows
while in labor, giving birth
to calves of beauty,
Never knowing she was smiling,
Spreading star-burst sparkles
from her eyes.

DRESSING TIME, PLAYING TIME

I could dress time up like a whore,
stockings ripped
Or I could gild her with my own
made spun gold
I could fold time up like an accordion
and play chords in unison with
everyone else
Or should I play a solo?

PUCK AGAIN

I was born of mustard seed
Milkweed fluff I floated from
I will sneeze a ragweed tune
My home the paths that lead to dreams
I have sworn to no one here
I am lost in nothing seen
I have wandered to the elf
and green wart lichens hide me
Wealth is forms I made myself
Tiny forest glades, my space
I find life in cobweb sheen
and world can't roar within my ear
I stop to comfort lost cocoons
Small caught threads I halt to mend
in my loom inside my eye of wonder
I am weaving fairy homes
I repair the broken wombs
Hope of flying my delight
I will whisper to the wings
and cry with joy with their release
until in height of many colored ecstasy
I break
and disappear with wind breath
disappear with angel hiss
down my magic night.

NOT TAME

I'm not tame yet
and will not bend
or genuflect
or try to put a name on
why I stretch...
My long long limber leap
a nameless leap
to capture love
a catalyst to dream
to resurrect, to resurrect

I won't hinder me
who grabs the flower I have made
who dabs the rhythm of the days
with my airborne sweets

Winds of wrath blow by me
My weightlessness transcends the fury
of a hundred galaxies

GOING HOME

When you squeeze the wet
from the delicate lace of the web
in the sunlit grass
Slide down the dew soaked lawn
Saunter in and out of the
reeds by the pond
Splatter yourself into water beetles
Splash through the nests of toads
without letting them know
Go at an unmeasured rate
through sun blinks
Flow the flitter to the wings
of dragonflies
Hide under turtle shells
When you play the sunset until it glows
to dusk
You'll be home.

ALIGHT ON A LIGHT FOOT

Regardless of the heavy blue black smoke
on the highway,
even though the snow is smudged with coal dust
and refuse lies in between my thought and you,
still I will hear, sing, alight on a light foot,
get you to tune a string to move a light foot,
and I will roll a golden ball down the highway

Even though the snow is black with soot,
the ravens white with ash
the bellies of rockets swollen
with stinking fuel,
the children's wings folded
I will send a beam out
blow the bluebirds alive
sit on a tree limb for days and days
and paint the green in spaces between
your eyes and mine

THAWED STARS

Will you be satisfied with thawed stars
or will you demand fresh ones?
I'm not sure if fresh ones are available
or freshly killed, or frozen;
How do you like your stars,
well lit? dim? lightly chilled?
I don't have electric ones.
Five pointed stars are out of style,
archaic
Stay awhile and I'll find one less
blinding.
I've dipped scores and scores of my stars
in black paint so as not to offend
We must placate placate
A world of men wearing sunglasses
But beware of thawed stars
They drip.

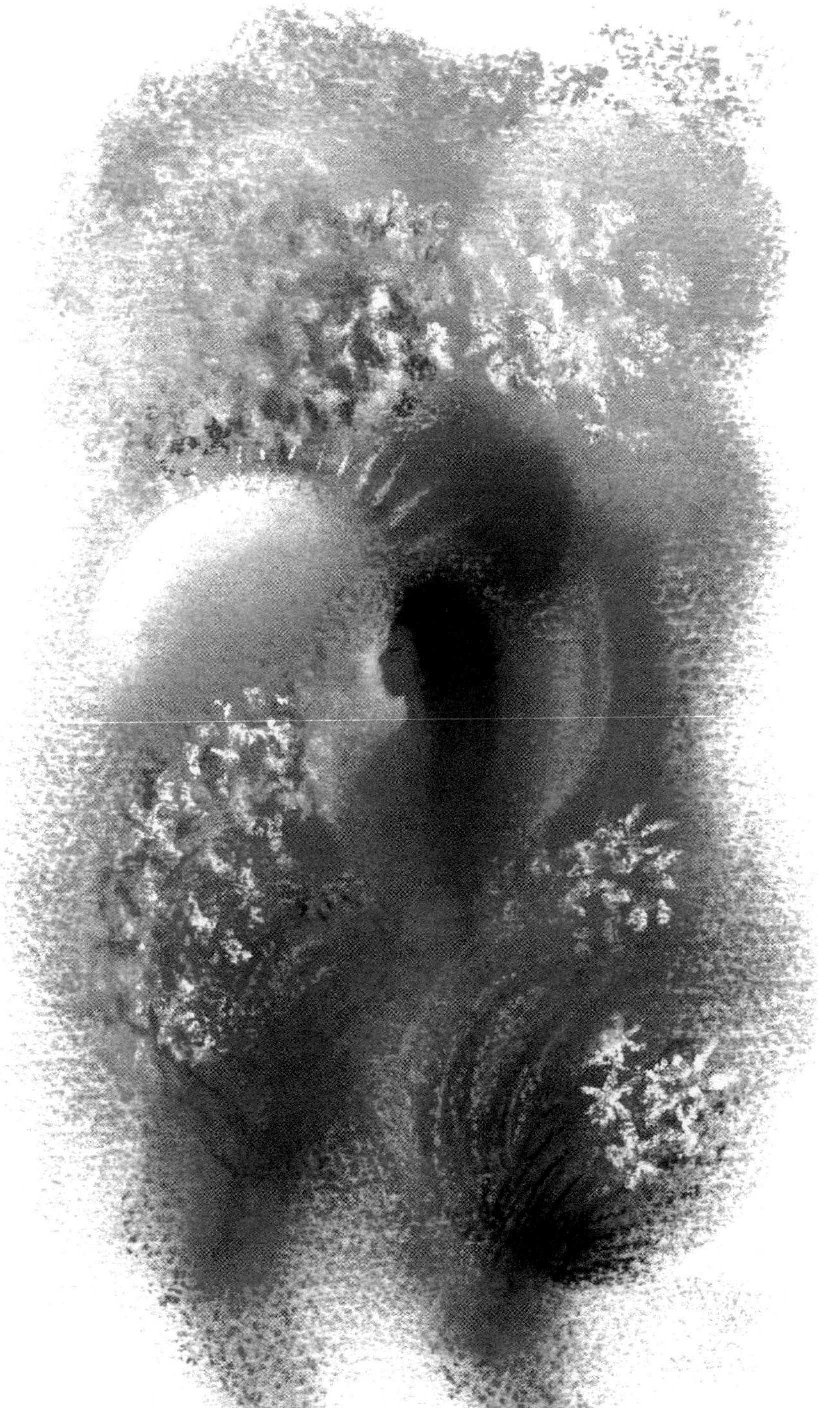

Chapter Two

Breathless Love

DENIAL

It can't be, it can't be!
I am going through a raindrop
into you
Let's deny it for awhile
I need a yawn or two
to remind me I'm on two feet
to keep earth the proper distance
Rain is wet and you are you
I'm not ready for a fling
that makes me live in leaves
and things.

MATING

This planet, so small,
I fall into you
making dreams fast,
past someone's crusty energy,
Lost and left in yesterday's
pretended space.
We fly.
Let's make a space for
tulips redder than colliding suns,
Our lips will meet in centuries we make
for lengthening the fun
of mating in the sky.

I FIND YOU

I cannot have you, mundane,
french-fried in a Woman's Day microwave.
I cannot see you in a doormat, impeccably
displayed, or on a perfect roof-top.
For I am finding you in a place
that has no scope or limit.
I find you in serenity, a leaf not formed
or set.
You are carried on my child's sleeve
Her smiles are your adornment.

CALMNESS

What am I doing in this calmness?
I could make a wild frenzy of
racing leaves dance,
but I sit here in a pool of love,
motionless
Why not throw frenetic rhythm
and gallop stars?
Contented to parley with nothing,
I'm not even bending knees.
You could move me if you tried.
Just show me your eyes.

WHAT EFFECT?

If I dye my hair red
will you love me then?
If I tint this shell yellow
put thin lines of green
under both knees
follow the lead of avant-garde fashion
pile foam in airy ringlets
on a flying hat
fly silver pins 'round my belly
line my navel with tiny purple roses
hide in a wig of spun gold
will this ignite your passion?
Undressed I am a pale illusion
As plain as I am
in thin disguise
You do not see me shining, burning
through my simple eyes.

PERIODS OF RAIN

There were periods of rain
mixed with you
growing sunshine in your
garden smile,
blue rain mixed with
silver laugh
over that mountain
I saw you there
Snowing here, but
you were hoeing daffodils
in your garden mountain home,
raking piles of apple blossoms
flowing from your
garden smile

NOVEMBER WEATHER

"There were periods of rain mixed with you..."

Inside body heat
pushes me
to grab
particles of cold
Icicles
fall
in crackling heaps
and I jump in
but still
I burn
thoughts making puddles
slow drips
You say
you hate the rain

IN MY PERFECT LANDSCAPE

I took you in my acres green
through long summer's yawn
and found you in the leaves
unfurling,
waiting in the dawn I'm making
Can I see you in that perfect tree,
caressed with interlacing green?
A spot of you in a sparrow's throat
in radiance of sun gleam,
blending with me over here
in my loving eye

SUNFLOWERS

Pulling myself up
and condensing myself to a point,
I threw an explosion of sunflowers
into you waking up over there,
yawning,
the yawned smile just wide enough
to receive
my brilliant display.

DOWN THE BALUSTRADE

Cascading down the balustrade
careening around the corner
caroming from wall to wall
crinkling up and straightening
out again
your smile finally did a dance
that landed right in the middle
of mine.

BREATHLESS

I am breathless to you
  nothing to you
I will make a mountain for you
I am open to you
  nothing to you
  is a barrier
Waste some green space with me
Hop with new feet to me
Turning backwards is a track I find
distasteful
Let's begin again
I make birds sing
You can face me; nothing is me
Everything

STATISTICS

What's your gross income this week?
Did you make a new newmometer for smiles?
Graph the delighted shiver of each child
as you touched him
with a light beam?
That slow slide downward on your trombone
that made six women weak in the knees...
was it recorded on your statistical register?
Can I count the number of ways
your love banged me around in a swoon,
immeasurable,
except by the fathomless rule of your eyes?

MORE BIRTHDAY WORDS
for Mark

I filled some pages
with thick wholesome words
like milkshakes, like that chocolate cake

You thought it was only to flatter you
and bowed shyly
Words are not sticky and I wrapped them
in ribbons
We went round and round and round
Our silliness the only thing that mattered

You took out lexicons and crafted trees
of ecstatic arcane vocabularies
Computers can't giggle, but they
can listen carefully
and grow fat with digits

We horse around all night, stuff ourselves with
new ways to do nothing at all,
I'm sure there are more

I have no reason to roll myself in more ink
it just feels good
and that old ratty chair has so much to say

Complexities are just laughter that got folded
into too many folds, filed away accidentally
and misplaced
A puzzle of a frown folds neatly too,
adding to the pile

You remembered to be reborn and then went to sleep
dreaming of unbirthdays
while my smile stayed awake all night
visiting children, carrying the soft dark air
like a cloak

TIPSY

I sit in your smile and
the walls fall down
We find reasons for tangents
and digressions
into flying tapestries and
woven trapezes
The riddle of my last frown dissolved

You rainbow me alive
into lengthy dissertations
on floating leaves, theses on
the transparent nothingness
of a flower

I become learned in a second
of leaning into you
Heartbeats mixing outside
the sweat of reality

Our tiny potent thoughts swell
and the universe
tips over

CHILDREN ARE TAUGHT...

Children are taught
backwards and forwards
upwards and down
Yet clearly the whole world
is motionless
in their one glance
of pure wonderment

SHED SKIN

A child's clothes dropped
on the floor
Piled crumpled refuse
The shed skin of play

Chapter Three

The Evidence

BREAK OF DAWN

After the break of dawn
I stepped in the pieces
all day

THE ANTIQUE CHAIR

I have been waiting for my poems to lie flat on the page,
even descriptions of a placid leaf on a summer day,
contemplation of the rungs of an antique chair,
wooden, calm, round, evenly notched.
Leaves not flying over rungs in a careless phantasmagoria;
carvings, neat, not turning into mysterious runes,
nothing swaying wildly.
I am sure the moment will come
when the piercing notes of another world will no longer
penetrate
and I rest in quiet.
I am studying the long even boards on the porch floor
and I ignore the frantic rhythm of bees,
rapid heartbeat of hummingbirds.
Will this bring me the satisfaction of growing old?
To have the dedication of the somber swept front steps
without raging interference
Wind of my invention.

TOLUCA LAKE SPRING

Flowers, so sweet, the smell clings to the skin
Sidewalks glitter, grow mica
The sky coughs a dry haze
Distant mountains slow to a brown crack

Women pull neon skirts out of closets
High heels scratch cement walkways
Cats shed houses like fur
Houses fling open their shut eyes
then close them tight
Air conditioners are revving up their engines

The days aren't ready to be smothered in smog
They are still pretending real clouds
They blink patches of blue

The hard ground resists my spade
The sycamore has finally decided to clothe himself
after a long winter's nakedness
Ivy, clipped to a neat edge, waits politely for a drink
Palm trees stare straight ahead as usual

Blenders whip up strawberry froth near open windows
There are those breezes, can't make up their minds,
hot? cool?
Gardeners blow away bird songs
Poets put the roar of blowers into poems

The flowers are playing sweet silent violins
Profusion of confusing pastel sounds
Little old ladies take their cars for walks around the
block,
find pennies to buy eggs
My head cracks open, sprouting poems

Hormones bend logical minds
Leaves are jealous, watch for starlets in tight pants
Trees are getting it up in green fast before the coating
of smog dulls their senses
Smog, LA's permanent excuse for irony

My old car grins and winks
We ride to Pasadena to find the real spring

SMALL ACCOMPLISHMENT

Today I failed to leap
out of a night
of exploding dreams

I did not crash down
the disappearing stars,
nor race out to wrinkle the sun,
crack the blue plate
of the sky

My slow lumbering thoughts
yawned me awake

I walked out blinking
in the morning light,
surprised by a sprig of goldenrod
to put in my small blue china vase

CARETAKERS

The material universe isn't polite
It doesn't clean up after itself,
say "please" or "thank you"
and it thinks nothing
of leaving odors behind
Many people spend years trying
to civilize the inanimate,
build tall straight buildings of glass
and little golf carts
They are satisfied that these things
don't speak
even when spoken to
and never think of this
as simply bad manners
They are satisfied that the glass buildings
sparkle in the sun
the chairs can be sat upon
and the golf carts hum
That these things fail to say hello
isn't notable or expected
Yet I think it's odd that we
are all such careful caretakers
of the dead

ON THE TRAIN

Through the eye of
a rectangular window
Dozens of white triangular sails
come closer
A passel of ghosts having conversations
on the water
My eyes on the train
passing
two quickly
My ears too slow to hear

TRUCKS

The tractor trailer truck
hurls itself down the highway
with a rumbling density
that shocks the world
out of grace
I try to let the vibrations pass
as though I were invisible
and create a universe for trucks
to be in
or come from
The universe of trucks
with greased intensity, battered tongues,
angle plates and heavy overgrown men
who shatter windows with their tread
The women weigh in by ton
and satisfied with a night of groans
the men lumber out again
to haul crash pull the trucks,
hit the road
crossing huge boulders, hurling wrenches,
heaving their heavy world bit by bit
into place.

THE EVIDENCE

When all the words fall
into place
the missing parts of my life
will become tangible
real evidence
documented skyscrapers
known sidewalks and trucks

When all is said and done
the hard facts will be in
No one will dispute
scientific documents
verifying the real existence
of my left toe
and other important accouterments

No one will doubt
the solidity of this very
unshifting truth

But by then I will be gone
ringing in a thousand sonnets
singing to a million
invisible ears

STILL LIFE

A parched region of wall
holds a metallic picture of a rose
framed by a mirror reflecting
heavy velvet colored drapes
and dirty rose colored blinds
The rose in the picture is backed up
by two smaller ones
That part of the wall is in shadow
but the pink of the roses
glints outward
like the pink foam at the bottom
of a Tequila Sunrise glass
when you've had one too many

The sagging couch is brown
and the rug is blue, abused by
feet and spilt ashes
The streaked sky turned upside
down and emptied there
a firmament with a lost identity

The dead-eyed rose cannot fade

A large glass hand-painted lamp
has no bulb and gives no light
The shade is tilted sideways
an accident of some careless hand,
moving to turn on the tv
in search of a passionate conversation,
eyes matching eyes
wit matching wit

or merely a casual bit of chatter
the rose just sleeps through

TRAFFIC LIGHTS

Hardly any traffic
on a Sunday morning
but those traffic lights
hang there anyway
Little round-eyed hoods
changing colors faithfully
for no one at all
Blank beacons complacently
swaying gently in the wind
You want to improvise
Dance through and signal them
Let them know their numbers
have been rearranged
But they just blink
on and off to the empty roadway
Green yellow red
Green yellow red
And you wonder what they see
Maybe another whole universe of cars
they can switch on and off automatically

WAITING ROOM I

The man laughed when I suggested
his beard might grow and be interwoven
with his tie,
which looked like a tapestry.
The woman sitting next to me gave
a short nervous giggle and turned away.

WAITING ROOM II

The seat had been chosen deliberately
to accommodate
perfectly clean white sneakers
well-pressed neatly hemmed blue jeans
hair clipped in straight lines
a purse containing no loose gum wrappers
nicely shaped eyebrows

Seeing me writing this
the impeccably organized parts
were picked up
and quickly carried away.

MY MOTHER

My mother fell
small and wrinkled
on the morning
and the moon slipped
off into some hidden darkness

Coffee steamed us awake
and the cups chattered
in the cupboard

My mother dropped
like an ancient stone
into the blue light
of dawn

The day rolled out
like a newspaper
with tiny important print
we had to read
to know

My mother
heaved away the sky
left clouds loaded
with rain

There would always be enough
for flowers
we could grow

My mother left the kitchen
covered
with cups and papers

We were dizzy with words
We drowned in heavy milk

We lay muffled
like shifting sand
curious with the weight
of dreams
waiting for the delicate
shadow of the moon
to release us back
into buoyant darkness

THE BOY

I watch the rush of leaves propelled by wind
and pushing in one fierce
formation, an army in rout ravaging the gutters
under a darkening sky
The dried skeletons of asters
shake and drop the last
of their seeds
Marigolds stand on blackened stalks
Their yellow blooms, still vibrant,
stare, the frightened eyes of last survivors
Even the weeds decline
Doubt, decay fill my mind
I am in curious agreement with the elements

I watch a small boy achieving
the top of the hill
Backpack carried, light as a wish
Proud, he comes from school,
wearing the autumn wind like a scarf,
he dangles weeds from his legs
and casts the clouds back,
out of the way of the sun
A light comes from his eyes
and autumn, which had brought me down,
now shines in colors, red, rust, orange
The chaos of the past moment gone,
as the boy, bright alive
shakes leaves flowers weeds
in a second of laughter dissipates the gloom.

THIS FLAT SCREEN

This screen is so flat
why do giant feelings jump out of it?
wiggling rolling wishes
and invisible people

Dogs snore in 3-D with real noses
and real tongues and heavy breathing
that keep you up at night

But the screen is flat and
the one I have is only black and gray
conjuring nothing
lying there in no one's way

Women in skirts rustle
men smell of heavy work and
the kitchen kettle screams

But the screen is flat
and yet something is always happening
I feel the sorcery of it
I am completely fooled

away from the loud birds
windows with light streaming in in the morning
large flowers in fields

I want to jump into the screen
find fingers, toes, people with long arms
I want to grab the screen
turn it into an origami paper

Make a paper swan covered with computer poems
cover myself with whomever is inside
paste myself into a book

Become an ocean of digits, forget I love
so much the flat screen or who is in it

EDGES I

Hot edge of sidewalk burns
until sight flies up to
thin sketches of buildings
tightly drawn against blue
of sky

Brick holds eyes of windows
antennas rise, needles
that pierce the invisible air,
air drawn upon by
architects

Long gone who built hodgepodge
brick glass and stone edges
sharp delineations
that rule my vision
with ragged lines

That stretch and bend up down
unfathomable reach
sight leans into and out
tries to find the end or
the beginning

When brick stone and chrome
first met the sky

EDGES II

The edges of trees lie against the sky,
irregular green lace
I can barely trace with my finger from
a distance
Closer, the crab apple hangs down
with a disorderly grace,
edges blending with the distant trees,
crispness blurring
as I look through the porch screens
rows of rectangles whose edges have a purpose,
or at least one I can immediately grasp,
straight and orderly.
From my corner I can see the spiders' webs
There are so many on this summer porch
or else my eyes are fooling me, looking through
the webs and the dust at the clear straight
lines of the windows
A sudden burst of wind is mixing in the ragged
patterns of the far-off trees
The trees wave, retreating and bowing
I don't know if this dance is what they were
born for
or just to baffle the eye,
as it tries to measure
within the narrow confines of rationality.

THE DUST AND THE FLOWER

Inside the plastic flower lies
a piece of dust
dust immune to busy hands
that clean and wipe and dry
A solitary mote
speaks to no one

Inside the plastic flower
little flies
cannot alight
The room's motion
cannot penetrate
No one asks why
or wherefore

If the plastic flower dies
limp and folded over
in the night
Will the dust arise to free itself
in flight?

No one asks
No one cares
for dust

THE EMPTY CHAIRS

The empty chairs
stand at the table
frozen at attention
waiting in permanent patience
for a bit of conversation
from absent masters
perfectly silent
immutably straight
with absolute humility
and no complaint

The empty chairs
hold position clear
with unspoken authority
and knowledge
of future human conclaves
not complacent,
yet knowing their place
and keeping yours for you
not forgetting
or remembering
so you can have the pleasure
of doing so

CAR POEM

Take the carburetor
bend it into six parts
Take the gas pipe
Turn it into a long tree stem
Take the spark plugs
Take the brake line
Drip it out
Take all the metal, the rubber, the chrome
Put it in backwards and upside down
Take in exhaust fumes, turn them all into ink
Wrap the windows in tin foil
Turn the wheels into fire
Accelerate backwards
Wrap the car up in a giant pink bow
Show me a good time in the back seat
Make my thin skin ripple
The whole thing falling apart
under magic moonlight
Dip the fenders in hot fat, bubbling with fries
Take me home in a wild wind storm
Smiling at all the other cars

THE MOVING PHOTOGRAPH SOMETIMES WITH SOUND

I wander along the narrow stretch
of black asphalt, the street
speckled with the shadows of trees,
the moving patterns, like restless
sleepers,
And push my way past men in suits
who gesticulate and talk excitedly
A small red car, blaring rock and roll
passes, bearing a teenager with tousled hair
He's grooving to the beat
Suddenly the car is gone,
a little splattering of indecency
in the quiet
Down the sidewalk a father
tows his frowning child home
early from school
Maybe she swallowed too many words whole
without digesting
Another car, large and white, creaks
as it lurches unevenly into a parking place
in front of a church,
then waits dutifully for half an hour
for a soul to emerge from the church door,
perhaps wondering why the squat body
of an old woman comes out instead
No one sees me
in my wandering down the sun-patched street
I am somehow invisible,
never disturbing
the moving photograph.

THE RELIGIOUS ACCOUNTANT

Speaking to him I noticed
the mole on his chin
The words fell from his mouth
into part of the carpet
I wondered if he occupied
that small spot on his face
or his right eyebrow perhaps
He seemed only a fragment
busy inside an insolvable series
of digits
a billion billion numbers
He held untold ciphers
inside a small body
that he was, he thought, only
a part of.
His "spirit," he said, was
somewhere "there"
an internal organ
coming alive
according to his calculations
and joining his God
once he was dead.

RIGGED DEAL

It's a rigged deal
You're in the basement
thinking that light bulb is the sun
Your ripped jeans, part of a suit of armor
Your bald pate, a shining coiffure
Your dirty sneakers, winged sandals
That cold cup of coffee, a bubbling glass of champagne

You'll soon wake up
You're in the sky, thinking that meteor is a slow moving rock
Your flying sparks, a sizzling marshmallow on a campfire
Your brilliant wings, small shadows on a dirty wall
The great expanse of space,
the whitener in your coffee cup

So now...
How does it feel to be sitting right in the middle of that waterfall at midnight?

IN A FIT OF DISTASTE

In a fit of distaste I withdrew
to avoid all things square triangular or fat
when perhaps I should have merely slurped them up
tat for tat.
With a modicum of scorn
I renewed my own little niche
a fine fleecy spot
neither thin nor square
I knew no one would find me here...
There, a somewhat erratic battle
with angles cuts sliding parts
irregular disjointed smeared.
Each side must fit, carpenter's rule
We are taught to bend a bit
to abide and not to stare.
I should show the room its own veneer
Paint the shellacking with one eye cocked
Could the walls quake with the thought
I might disown them?

POEM ON TOOLS

I grow sturdy and fat, studying the rules of this universe
I'll master yet the long and short of it, lines and dots,
exact measurements you can fold up and put in your coat pocket
I won't wreck my ship on the shores of inexactitude, love or mush
I shall be impervious with my fine metal rule
No rush to any death
I have placed my micrometer on each tool that comes my way
I have the steady look of one who knows arithmetic
and will not hurl myself into anything indescribable or lush
It is all explainable in my book,
a steady ballast for my passionate ship
on my mad mad sea of dreams

PEONY

I laughed into my broken flower
It awoke
I spoke peony
It shattered its tears on me
Crying crying
trying to be whole

THE PIECES

Is all this motion
the motion of souls
bent on restoring quiet?
The frenetic groping to gather
the pieces of the whole
like the priceless blue plate
dropped in a careless moment
from the cupboard
where it had rested peacefully
for millennia
We lie shattered.
Now you see us running
quotidian, almost in circles,
but never quite completing
the cycle
except to lie comatose
for brief periods,
(There are beds.)
The frantic rhythmic breathing
of crowds
push pulling the subways back and forth
The crush of bodies in Grand Central Station
Each soul going somewhere
You know they have a reason.
Bodies move, eyelids flutter up and down
Hands continue to grasp the handrails of escalators
Mouths mutter often unintelligible
but audible patter
Denials retorts blinks ugly stares
are there also
But mostly it's motion
even at desks.
Do they know there are pieces?
Can they remember the whole?

WITH VERY GOOD REASON

dedicated to The New Yorker

I will pen
fancy dialogue
between distracted diners
in tuxedos
and their estranged spouses
Stories that give class
to divorced gay psychiatrists
and their alcoholic kin
I will pen diatribes by dilettantes
who date debutantes
and have acid garden parties
I will pen
discussions of the good old days
in antebellum South
Descriptions of the dipsomania
of certain Yuppies
always implying inherent
antinomy
in each inevitable crisis
I will never mention
the one night I spent
all alone
hugging the moon.

ILLICIT BUSINESS

What right have you
to practice poetry
without a license?
You have not even applied
at the Office of Poetic Affairs
No, you left your thumb print in the air
Your daily dallying in trees
to pull and paint unsanctioned descriptions
remains unrecorded
And no one knows exactly
where your leaves will fall
Unregistered, unrestrained,
your license would have been suspended,
were you apprehended
Your dance, so undisguised, so free
of catalog, formation,
flies in no haste, in irregular
defiance of regulations, rules
Your lines remain in weightless books
And were they detected, they would
have never been selected
for important processes,
such as filing.
No, you were just pretending,
thinking you could avoid
the inevitable ending,
Caught, bent, folded and spindled.

YOU HAVE A RIGHT

You have a right to sit cross-legged in a bar and to shout loudly to your companion, blowing cigarette smoke in the faces of persons walking by.

You have a right to drag your first boyfriend into every conversation, to roll your eyes as you eat spicy Mexican food.

You have a right to drop your fork on the floor, to order pasta and oranges that aren't on the menu, to rebuke the waiter because he wasn't born in Guatemala.

You have a right to forget the name you had before you were born, to ignore the genius of six unknown poets, to juggle invisible apples, to write brilliant sonnets all night long.

You have the right to spurn someone as lover, to regulate yourself to fit old habits, never overgrown.

You have a right to sing out of tune, to jump in the aisles of theaters, to visit shows you once were star of, to not know the distance to the moon.

You have a right to silence those who scorn you, dig for crystals in deep caverns, roll your dice to make your fortune, to create a paradise that at this moment doesn't have a form.

You have a right to walk quite briskly, to light a candle, douse yourself in water that is freezing or water that is warm.

You have a right to dance in rhythms you made now or some you made in moments long gone.

You have a right to ignore the ridges of dark corridors, places you would rather place in your closet of the unknown.

You have a right to wrinkle all your shirts, to appear beautiful or desperate or forlorn.

You have a right to ignore your enemies, to paint the heavens many colors, to stand up as a beacon in the night, to warn me of your coming, to be blessed or to be damned.

You have a right to place a distance between the place you know is safe and the place there is a storm.

You have a right to say goodbye and a right to say hello...a piece of you always in each moment.

You have a right.

ARITHMETIC

Ten birds on a telephone wire
Two fly off
One decides to peck his feathers
Three remain perfectly still
Three more fly off
One more arrives and he is staring straight at the
absolutely blue sky
Four birds on a telephone wire
Three are thinking about dinner
One is dreaming
Two are listening to one bird's thoughts
He has four hundred and twenty-five thoughts
The others subtracted three thoughts
Nine birds on a telephone wire
Six fly off
Three birds keeping track of traffic
How many cars?
How much exhaust?
How many windows rolled up against the cold?
How long can you sit and count the birds?

AROUND THE CORNER

Around the corner
a rusty sound
Horses sprout wings
That manure plop is lit by sun,
an iridescence of colors
I angle back to find another me
Round about, sideways slant
Curved and rigged to go from
ragged to rich
from real to irregular
from astounding to the dullest of dull
My flat shoes sink into a spike heel hole
I look for a ghost in a shopping mall
Find a piece of coal in a silk stocking
Right corner turn
No, I won't go straight
I'll recompose myself into a tin symphony
after brilliant chords disappear
I won't fade into a sunset
I will light it up
with crooked light in a tiny filament
going in a zig zag in a dark room
I am looking around the corner

IN SLIGHT PROTEST OF MUPPETS

I am not immune to the sight of a plain tree
out in the open air,
yet I paint it streaked, curled and the cows
I see are not of the domestic variety
Three small flecked toads do not satisfy
my wandering eye
They must bark, in perfect sixths
Muppets are too real; they do not appear
and disappear without a trace
There are strings
And gadgets
Oh roll with me down my hillside
It is fairly slippery and is made of vibrating
flute tones, low and soft
A color of plums will float you aloft
Your keel is as steady as grapes on a still day
I am not pacified by the sound of tolling bells,
flowers, shapes entombed in real
From them there's no escape.

MY RED BALLOON

Inside my red balloon
atrocious
rain storms of quiet tinsel
coated in my own silver
slippery and never used
only atrocious because
you are yelling outside
Don't try and meet me halfway
Impossible
It's mine
inside
my red balloon

SPACE

Space is convenient
I know I am not you
Nor are you me
We don't trip over
one another
Our smiles don't get
all tangled up

Chapter Four

Lost/Found

THIS ISN'T ENOUGH

This isn't enough
It won't hold your attention
There are no explosions
flashing lights
dynamite, mad mad dances
This poem is only
the fall wind
fall passing in the air
through lips
scarcely there
hope in a shadow
a window reflection of you
a small breath
a faint reminder of the
complexion you had in summer
a faded painting
a yawn at supper
old folks' banter
before the long sleep
This isn't enough
to wake them.

ONE BAG

If I could put all that I owned in one bag
I would place one guitar
and I can't even play
I would put the sensation of your smile
the memory of that child sitting on the edge of a chair
with an ice cream cone, dripping
I'd put the arrogance of a Spanish dancer's arched back
seven flute tones before they disappeared in the air
a hundred blank pages
I'd put the poem that would win your heart (unthinkable
joy)
I'd put a map of places to place our dreams (inexhaustible)
I'd put points to place distances to own
all the future places to place
as many bags as I wanted

FOUND POEM

Random messages float in the air
like dogs making slurping noises
waiting for their masters
and we strain to hear
Some smell like bothered skunks and
we avoid them, close our car windows

A woodpecker calls to us from his rotten tree
The bullfrog has plenty to say
The poky donkey makes us pull him along
Old people take notes to remember and
repeat questions over and over
Who finds these poems and writes them down?

Or over there
as the Great Blue Heron takes flight
from one tree to the next
warning the woman in the canoe
of a coming message
she would have to snatch from the sky

Perfectly formed, like his wings
spread in a whoosh, flying soundlessly
the poem is looking for its landing place
under that turtle's furtive head
darting back into the water
What should be said?

Here or there or anywhere?
A small impression formed from dew
on early morning grass, a plop the cat left
a hundred different insects
the fox on the hill
or maybe just the thought of you

A rumbling starting in my head
a trembling hand
a motion to retrieve this song
before the sound is lost
an excited jitter, a flutter of joy
as the mind takes hold

Of what can't be held or
caught
A spider's work is easier to keep
her threads more taut
than this fleeting moment
that can't be found in a photograph

But can be seen in invisible ink
or in the pounding rain
You cannot hesitate or it is lost
It has no cost but fuels my heart
An endless source that disappears
and comes again with simple thought

THE LOST THOUGHT

I lost the thought years
after I had wound it
in the intricate blanket of desire
The threads of want, reject,
the woof and warp, the winning, losing,
dimming eyes, connecting in an
embarrassment of endorsements,
periodically followed by unwillingness
The thought at best guessed at
The unwieldy covering admired and analyzed
for snippets of information
The push the pull of want dried to crusts
Once bright integument
now mostly subject
for a passionate argument
to find the thought
I lost.

THOUGHTS ON AN OLD THEME

When the tree falls in the forest
I am crying in my kitchen
When the crow squawks
on a distant mountain
I am stumbling in a dark room
When a rabbit scurries
into its hidden hole
I am groping for a poem.

Who is listening to us?
Must he tell us we exist?

SKIN I

I have layers and layers of skin
to shed
I lie muffled and silent
under these dead coverings yet
I am reluctant to shed them
remembering how warm I was once
in the company of an ancient overcoat
I was snug in shining ermine,
radiant in mink
It was surprising to have this
integument cling
but it was my own doing
being so fond of covering things
I became an unconscious guest
captive within
an elaborate mansion of skin.

SKIN II

I lie
in acres of skin
and you do not even
wonder why
or consider whether
escape is possible

I should say that we
occupy these acres
but I was a bit shy
and you never asked
for my opinion anyway

You never asked me
how to fly
out of these fossil shell
bodies
and who am I to give advice?

You say
you don't have acres of skin
only a few feet or square yards
You spent some time measuring it

To die is simple
Many do it daily
from yards of skin
No one is giving advice
on flying
They'd rather admire
the landing places

VOYAGE OUT OF OLD SKIN

Until I had crawled out of the hole
fear lapped at my ankles
like old soup

I was sure I would arrive at some
distant shore eventually
so I read my maps
and sweated feverishly at night

Mornings were better
when newsprint seemed new
and coffee was reheated

Traffic was an interesting battleground
I had forgotten the old wars

There was never any snow here
and vacant lots full of stones
hid wildflowers

No one really cared about the tiny things
So I made my battles huge
so they might be real to someone

The sun was so far away
It burned anyway
and people shed bodies
as easily as snakes dropped skins

One little note got my attention
and I listened to it for a hundred years
but I missed everything else that happened
and a few people were mildly annoyed

Children were loud and woke me up
I decided it was better to play
more notes, be amazed at sunflowers

start over, drawing thin lines
that would startle someone into
the kind of laughter that lasts

SMOKE

In your smoke a gum wrapper
has become important
a casual glance smolders
the bottle of Snapple glows
with a strange unnatural glow

In your blurry cigar haze
a cup of coffee is a vat of ink
my hair a platinum wig
your few words, a love sonnet

In the wispy darkening air
the hard floor softens under my feet
ugly chairs float upwards
poems form

In the half-light of the evening
my thought of you turns to neat computer print
the walls divest themselves of cracking paint
trunks of unwritten letters are dumped in my lap

In the laughing fume-filled night
bread crumbles on my plate
I fumble for my keys
rest easily in a cloud I cut with a knife

COMMUNICATION LAG

I sit in the chasm between your words
The pause, stretched like an elephant's
arabesque
a silence monumental
I will bridge the gorge with a thin
thread of thought
Span the gap
Warm the cold with a narrow sliver of wit
A fast dance over treacherous pits
No one's hopes dashed
despite the slow tongue.

SPANISH GUITAR

This day dawned in upside down light
A Spanish guitar trickled in
and I started writing with my left hand
The clear bright of my thoughts schooled my childish scrawl
and I was not ruled by day's heat
nor fooled by the crooked tracings
Hand followed in spastic glee
the unearthly melody
The day turned back upside up
My right paw grabbed control
My writing pad lightly trembled, then agreed
Thought leapt forward
on its path, inexorably

SELF DETERMINISM

Raggety scatterly wind
wreaks havoc on awnings
you forgot to fold up
bends me into new words

Raggety scatterly wind
wrinkles the pond
sends me scurrying for poems
to catch gusts
that blow me to
desire
poems to blast back
become a lover
in my own way

Not the wind's

Chapter Five

These Birches/This Sun

THE APPLES

I lean over on you
and the wind shudders
Trees stand at attention
Branches, startled awake
sway, dropping apples like
small bombs
the children rake away and eat
delicious fruit
They wonder at the fertility
of trees

GREEN HAS AN ATTITUDE

The green smears itself
against grey sky
and clutters everything with green
Green has an attitude
It takes over
It doesn't ask permission
Green slaps itself all over
Bushes trees grass creepy vines
People try to fight back by
painting houses white yellow and blue
by filling the air with dark smoke and smog
Building whole cities with only
a few trees
Crisscrossing the landscape with
industrial junkyards
no green would be caught dead in
No, what you don't realize is,
It's a war
Green's got an attitude
People have to show green
who's boss

THE EYE OF THE TOAD

To see through the eye of the toad
I relinquished my thrashing will
emptied the haste of a lifetime
to blink with slow profundity
my mind devoid of
extraneous frills
that would cause an irregular jump
or disturb my solid concentration
on catching a fly
Slow toad eye

AUDITION

Grey night slides
fast
over delicate fingers
of stars
who
peer into moonlit lakes
to decorate their
shining faces

Painted ladies, waiting
to audition
but fading quickly

Upstaged
by brilliant carnival
of dawn

BIRCH TREE TRILOGY

I

If you are tired
of the birch trees'
incessant conversation
you should go down the hill
hide indoors
watch every rerun
drink tea with aunts
uncles brothers and
all their shadows
fill the silence
with the babble
the birch trees
wouldn't listen to

II

Caught in the stillness
of birches
I am held prisoner
until released by a flutter
of passing birds

III

It is November
when the birch trees
take hold of me
white bark sketching
the thin cool air
slender bodies like silver dancers
caught in delicate poses
their leaning embrace offering
no explanations

a white ecstasy that came
with nakedness
unabashedly shining
in a sudden burst of sunlight
the conversations of branches
drowning out the faint crumbling
of leaves underfoot
their stark poems piercing the air
mysterious murmurings you want to hear
so much
you stand and wait,
forever, it seems,
to perceive bare
birch trees

THE BIRCH

The birch seeks its place
with a lean white, grey-white thin stretch
against the mountain
a search that moves with
the imperceptible motion
of things which cannot hurry,
but still will try to
fetch out a still truth
from the solid green hill

I sat and sat and tried to pull
the motion of the growing birch up and up
and I was caught in its silence
and patience
I felt my own outrageous haste
the lurching and gasping,
the fear and the endless chase
to make my mark against the heavy earth
in short allotted time
while the birch waits
and grows slowly up
with the stark white serenity
of accomplishment

BLIND TREES SING

Trees sing
blind
see songs
wear leaves to
keep cool
Trees make love
in long pollen notes
no one can notate

VAIN TREES

Trees see themselves in the pond
The sun shines the mirror
to a murky brown-green
The wind ripples its surface
Pond weeds hide parts of trees' limbs
Trees preen, pose and bend
to see themselves
Fuzzy shapes that glow on and off
Long almost iridescent forms
turn green then fall into shadow

Trees cry when darkness falls
Lie in each other's arms,
blind and dreaming,
until they find themselves again
in the morning sun
to cut their figures
in the water.

DROPLETS

Inside the house
no air currents
Outside the house
sky bluer than the baby's eyes
The storm window holds water in droplets
inside pane, outside pane
in between them
there is water, clear drops
and I can't look outside
I only see glass and water drops and
nothing moves,
outside or inside
I breathe the dusty air,
translate the blue through clear drops of water,
waiting for the sun to decide my next move.

CLOUDS

Smooth moving clouds
release me from
the monotony of blue

A little bit of gray
to cover too much brightness

Light shining through
Just enough to keep me awake
Just enough to remind me
of my next appointment

I'd like to follow who
is sending clouds across
the huge expanse of blue

I'd like to celebrate
the steady flow of wind
instead of waiting in
the blank space of light

I'd like a few droplets to fill my pages
a random scattering of
water to make my day
more willful

Under this scutter of weather
I'll find my own colors
and write what I meant to
instead of what the sun said

Paint in the gradations of gray
until blackness or back again to light
as I wish it

DIRECTIONS FOR LAUGHTER

Lift your laughter higher
slightly to the left
of the fading flower bed
Let it linger there
where the scent
of a leaf of dry lavender
moves in a tiny breeze
Pay attention
to your ripple of laughter
and what it tickles,
the moth flying through the air,
the wavering dragonfly,
the determined ladybug
might swerve
in the delicate waves,
forgetting direction and purpose
lost in your laughter,
flying to the wrong address
falling
dizzy
at your feet
in a flutter of confusion
So move your laughter slightly to the right
Hold it quiet
in that bed of contented sleeping roses.

DEBAUCH

Hearing the rain falling, falling, falling
I am drunk, soused
I am taller than the trees
wiser than the birds
I roar; there are no lions
I take the rain in teacups,
float in the pines,
forego the company of men
dine in flowers

Jumping in the rain rolling, rolling, rolling
in leaves dripping
I am under the influence, intoxicated,
totally wiped
I speak in tongues
Rattle on with toads and slip with underwater
tadpoles
I store moss under my stones
gloat with spiny things
down where no man has ever gone

Only fools know what I have known
I am drunk drunk drunk
in the sullen rain

Unclothe your creature comforts and come
You will lose yourself in the willing wet
You will forget
and remember
You will drink the rain

I NEED

I need
the steadying air
the comfort of the heady wind
rushing in the trees
The heavy heavy rain
whirlwind panicking leaves
unpredictable gusts
rough unfurling sheets of weather
pounding hail.

I need
the heat of the sun
the regular heartbeat of flowers
growing
The crawling snails
unfailing purple heather
gathering storms
the form of eddies, whirlpools
stirring fish in spawn.

I need
the pressure of the clear pond
the weight and measure
of the elements to hold
Such comfort drawn in patterns known
and me the watcher, willing this
since time long gone

LAWNS

Walking past the green square lawns
I find a perfect carpet
each blade upright and separate
not a spot of brown, even in early spring
the border cut to a geometric edge
like a gentleman caller
in a starched shirt giving a green lesson
in etiquette
It has the proper formula
and is following prescribed rules
I am always careful when I walk by
and always pass silently and respectfully.

But it is a relief
two houses down to find
that scraggly patch, crabby and spotted
with clover and dandelion
and that small leafed weed with tiny purple
flowers that look like violets
scattered and wild
cheerful noisy guests
I could talk with for hours.

WINDOW

Flat colorless panes
press away winter's glare
holding me fixed
wanting
a sprig of green
The window tempts me
with a smear of sunlight
Smudged panes stand between
my wishes
and
leafless branches,
the cold stare of empty streets

With eyes closed
I can leap
into the tight buds
of sleeping azaleas
right outside my kitchen window

MOON I

The moon reaches out
No sudden rays
A long sallow familiarity
A pension plan for lunatics
paid over millennia
The moon's rays
A soft lament
for lovers abandoned
in the light of it
The moon plays no part in it
unless we cast our thought
indicate the emotional drift
Cast our melancholy on
the push and pull
of the tides.

MOON II

The towering moon
walks on the water
in the tide
oblivious to centuries
rubbing its surface
Nature lies in its nubs,
unnourished, unrevived
by astronauts
who brought no flowers
Those caught in clandestine
love affairs hide
in the light of the moon
Their moon memories stalk them
Who makes the thoughts
for the moon?

MOON WARNING

When you rise to kiss the moon
do not lose yourself
in her craggy crevices or
flatten yourself on her smooth
contours

Keep your distance
lest you float into
moon's delirium

Do not ponder her thoughts
Ride in your own dimension
You have no need to tangle
in imponderable moon threads
or dance in her folly

When you rise to kiss the moon
consider only her craft
though she may astonish you
with her cool beauty
Admire the carvings of millennia,
the many faceted shards of her surface,
the intricate patterns of her nubs

But do not linger
in moon's heady swoon
or breathe her quivering air

Keep your eye calculating the radiance
Know the luna's luminating kiss
and steal away
before you are stolen
by moon madness

SORCERER

The sky holds no sorcerer
only me bent sideways
thinking I own the clouds
worrying over a rainstorm
fumbling with a spell to cast
on fresh clean laundry
hanging on the line

PARADOX

I want to be swallowed in one piece
by that giant oak tree
Branches carving shapes
in exquisite asymmetry
a complex crooked webbing
against the sky
I can be wrinkled tall uneven
mottled
I can grow awry bending upwards
I can be the ecstasy of green
emerging
Inside this tree
I find myself complete
daring the tree to be me and
knowing I can be the tree
in all its parts
Myself a whole
finding in the wayward tree
my own perfect simplicity.

RECKLESS

That tree is reckless
with its limbs
It doesn't care
which way it sends them
Those branches bending and weaving
first beckoning
then withdrawing send
messages to the wind
and the wind says,
"Go with me, one way."
But the tree stays in a wayward
confusion
holding me captive
in its crooked beauty

RAIN MOMENTS ON THE TRAIN

The water streaming down
the glass panes like
hungry tadpoles, tails growing
The boats docked
in the cold November rain
are silent
People mumble
under huge raincoats
The river is a prisoner
The heavy mist
has stuffed its gray gauze
into river's mouth, holding it hostage
We glide through the mist
saying nothing
like spies

REMEMBRANCE

I am not sure if I saw you last week
or before the temperature rose slightly
I do not retain time well
and tend to let it roll off
like water from a turtle's back
I'll be coming back in late March
when there is a point of remembrance
the crocus proving itself
against the snow.

LIGHTNING AND THE MOON

Slow moon's sullen gaze
falls down through lowering clouds

Skittery lightning
too fast
does his dance to mock the moon
who has no pull on lightning laugh

Bright flash in crazed glee
streaks the night with songs
plays tag with frightened clouds
dashes off witty tidbits
lashes the crying sky
hides in giggles behind rumbling thunder
calls the moon in inaudible shrieks
daring her to play

Moon stays oh so cool, oh
so cool
"No comment"
says the moon

SNOW I

Under the expanse of snow
the field lies brown and hard
Virgin beauty in reluctant
dormancy
It lies and waits

Under the shallow mantle
of complacency
I yield
wanting to be heard
The surging of my blood stopped
in stasis
I lie and ache

And who will push the bound up
earth apart
and break the clods
the winter froze
And who will urge
the pounding of my heart?

SNOW II

The snow makes the earth mumble
No more sharp, well-enunciated creaks
The birds' shrieks are muffled
into soft crinkles of sound
The blanket wraps bundles
of houses cars
Huddles them into quiet
A million particles of white
insulate the thunder
cushion the sharp edges of night

The snow makes silence right
A soundless expanse of serenity
covering every corroded part
in mute purity you can't see
but feel
Snow makes the earth fumble to move
suspends all thoughts of weeping
leaves us dumb and voiceless
in momentary innocence

RUMORS

They say that soon
the sun will be swept
into the sea
The moon will visit me
and tell me
how to rescue the sun

But I know these are only rumors

The sea keeps secrets in violent waves
and leaves me wondering

The sun burns alone
in scorching silence

And only I live to dream.

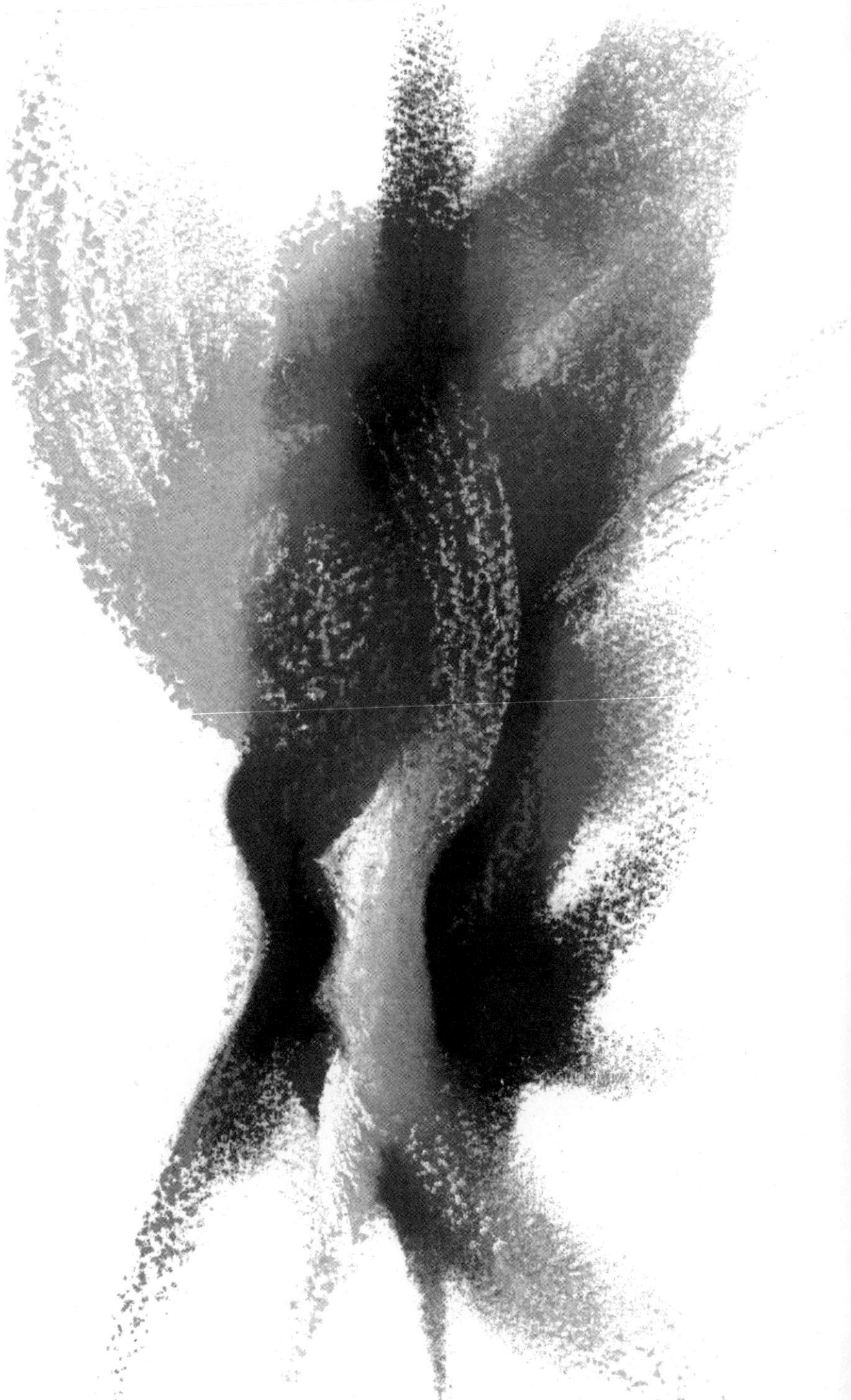

Chapter Six

The Joke's On Me

SWAGGERER

Translation please!
I'm lost in thistle tangledown raggedy
windy swaggerer's breath
tangling me up in twisted
convolutions of someone else's (not even
his)
hot and passionate breeze
I am ragged tagged torn about
Can't make out a note
in this whirlwind ragtime upside down jest;
The joke's on me, I guess
or him or her
We've forgot the point
And who started it?

SEA CHANTEY

Down at the shore the wind blew me a rogue
Sand snatched and knee whacked
and full to the tilt
of winking mischief
We daggered a dance
to a band of toe snapping crabs
and horsed our way into shoes we nabbed
from underwater belly whoppers
The day dawned hot
The night came cold
But nothing could stop
me and the rogue
The dagger toothed sidewinder
with winks in his shoes
and daredevil tantaggled
seaweed moods
Danced me up right out of this world
where down at the shore
the wind blew

WOMAN IN RED

She rose
and stretched
pulling her electric
beauty
over every limb
Morning became her
and she sent
volts crackling
down the wires
as she prepared
hair eyes lips
to meet the day
A cool flow
connected eyes
to steel
lips to red
fingertips to wheel
as she generated
sizzling energy
for car, road,
any passing man
to feel.

WAITING
for Bob Hart

Expecting to see you
I peered into the potent darkness
Did you step out to sweep the moon?
Are you putting a doorstop
on a swinging star?
Did you pause to ring Saturn's
gaseous bell?

In your absence
the darkness vibrates
penetrating my loneliness

Are you slicing bright yellow
lemons on a volcanic island
in the Pacific?
Preparing a perfect iced tea
in the shade of a bamboo
somewhere in China?
Dicing pomegranates and dropping
tiny ruby-eyed bombs
on quivering goldfish in Tibet?

I swim in the darkness
waiting

VISIT

I dropped in to see you
and felt beautiful
and invisible
I held the world
in my arms, green and
captive,
while you whistled
and tap danced
and wondered what that
breeze was

CONVERSATION

I opened my mouth to speak
and three white doves flew out
You laughed and clapped your hands
Long trails of ivy
grew around your ankles
You fell into the two immense oceans
of my eyes
I raced closer
Your heart stopped beating
but you were breathing
the seaweed that was pulling
you into me
I moved into a starfish
under your feet
Then seeing me inside
mother-of-pearl
you changed course
to entertain me
with small smooth stones
I made a tambourine of gulls
tapping their feet on the heavy sand
We joined hands
listening to the calls of oysters
the inaudible squealing of eels
I emptied my stories into the sky
You leaped to find them

THE FABRIC

I am sure that I would listen to you,

if I weren't sworn to finding

the fabric of me

   not in

blankets

newspapers

old bricks

black shuttered buildings...

I would be interested in hearing about the

   composition of

molecules

rusty chairs

even...raindrops

Except that I just sweetened the call of
that bird

without a single thing

CAST YOUR FUTURE

Cast your future in my direction
Throw the dice
It's a clean uncluttered flip
Skin doesn't count but could be included
Shake and shiver a little first
Find the die, the dying will just be
the trick of daring me to another race
No time wasted

Don't mind the broken glass
I'm filling them faster than clumsy
hands can drop them
Memory is just a paste-up job
and we'll be here way past closing time

No one will be left behind
A fast dance on top of barrels
of pent-up roses, barrels will split,
spilling a zillion petals
An orgy of flower perfume
won't spoil cherished rust

A billion particles of crazy ancient,
Touch-me, touch-me nots
aren't stored, aren't raising any dust
My storm a game you stir
to make another day light up
to destroy the past
to throw me past chance
onto one uncluttered page
where you cast the die
You decide

BURN THE KITCHEN DOWN

Oh burn the kitchen down
with its tidy aprons hanging on hooks
the shiny pans, the pretty nooks
the neat little lives of domestic bliss
Burn it all down, rub the ashes
in my breasts
Start a furious riot with incense and lust
Throw out the dustpans and brooms and such
Come to me shining in newly made armor,
pierce me with words, drown me in song,
with daggery dances you rip me apart,
a love-fooled muse you fill me with dreams
with lances of laughter, explosions of wit
Let's go and bury sanctimonious drips
the precious old patterns, the teacups
the dried up old muttering mothers and tits
that sacredly bled the milk for our flesh
Let's burn it all down with our glorious glee
There is nothing important but you
and yes, me!

ADVICE FOR WOULD-BE LOVERS

Before considering making love:

Shower yourself with lilacs, wearing heavy boots to keep from flying up into the petals.

Drink a cup of strong tea that has been laced with a potion to make you forget you left the kitchen on fire.

Run several miles until you are exhausted.

Forgo the company of people with small minds.

Conduct a rigorous examination of all files containing old love letters. Discard.

Dress neatly for a while, so you will not regret falling into the sweet disorder of undress.

Free your treasured collection of exquisitely pinned down butterflies.

Dine daintily on clean white meat for at least one week to prepare your palette for the red dripping juices of lust.

Use any available device to loosen held down dreams, real or imaginary.

Practice not doing as you are told, wearing your hat backwards and coming home very late.

Practice the art of awakening a sleeping body with hoarse love cries.

Press rose petals in a book as a memory of your former

orderly life.

Regret nothing.

Dispose of old tablecloths, ancient china and handkerchiefs containing dried tears.

Strenuously exercise the power of your wit to muscle you through the thick swamp of your desire.

Practice dancing, but only in front of a mirror, to admire yourself.

Sing the songs of a hundred birds, glisten with the sweat of race horses.

Take risks.

Undress slowly at night, admiring every part of your body, slip out of it.

Wear the darkness of night as your only clothes for seven nights.

Wear the brightness of the sun as a shirt for seven days.

Drink a cup of strong tea laced with a potion of remembrance of everyone you have ever loved.

Do not wait to find out that you are ready.

SIZZLE

Just one nibble and
I catapult headlong
into you as you stoke the furnace,
bake your crusty songs

Your temper sets the table
Tidbits from the fiery feast
drop, sizzle

I rest burning fish
in cool water
Float steaming teapots
in frozen milk

Your hot repast rolls
off my tongue
Flaming shark notes singe
Flavors mix in music blast

I'll fold snow over
a table lit by harps on fire
Wallow in a sunrise of sugar
Call for ice to crack

MOON MARMALADE

Buckets of moon marmalade
smother me
I wish to grease the sky:
fat of duck, crisp of pig

Sugar moon holds me captive
I eye oily chips, think of ways
to slick the table with a belly
dancing feast

I gasp for air in sweet moon essence
Laughing angels swoop in hordes
I hide from whirlwinds of
translucent beating wings

I dream of ways to deep fry
dazzling wing-tip fritters,
roll in saturated fat from
derelict roly-poly angels,
slip moon glow into fairy grease

Those doe-eyed noodles look
innocent enough
I wrap myself in starch
A carafe of wine offers escape

STICKY STUFF

Can you peel me off?
I am a poet
I stick invisible
push pull the thought to you
Can you throw me out?
Disposable rubbish
doesn't last long
might shine and crackle in the dark
Keep you up at night
You might try
to tear out my tongue
Poems flow with speech
But I sneak up on you in dreams
Throw color to
your pale paste-up dolls
Grin the park green
with off\on, on\off Cheshire cats
Nowhere is really safe
I hunt for vacant spots and fill them
Make emergency parachute jumps
into empty stares
Machine gun indifference
You can't match my fireworks
Can you snuff me out?
Who glows without light
Can you peel me off?
I sticky taffy pink
your sour blue bubble gum
warm honey gooey stuff
your own forgotten candy
made when you were still sweet
You can peel me off
but I will still find you
I am a poet

CERTAIN CONDITIONS

If I continue to say clever things,
you will flow me a penny
and I will sleep in the dark alone,
crying myself awake as I call your name

If I arrive dressed in mink,
the curl of lipstick, a temptation,
you will flow me a million dollars
and my sheets will be sweaty with
your exertions

If I sit quietly in a plain brown dress,
writing poetry in a corner,
you will stand politely, shake my hand
and recommend that I go with
the banker, the baker or the bricklayer,
the better to provide support

If I waft a scent of eyelash in your direction,
wink, and hint of inner moans,
you will buy me a drink and laugh at my little jokes
and twinkle diamonds into my lap

If I stand alone, worrying the surface of the moon,
you will pass by quickly, fearful of treading on my shadow

If I never tell you my name,
you will fall like a brilliant stone into my bed,
lie in a shining stupor, stroking my image

I will escape through the window
I will hold a small flower and wait

CLOTHES

Honestly, I can wear that jacaranda tree as a scarf
although I'm not sure if purple is my best color
You say, no, it's not true
You exaggerate
An oleander bush over each breast
will not ward off nibbling
That eucalyptus tree with peeling skin
would make a dainty hat pin
but you defer
Parrots in your hair?
The sky is my bonnet
Clouds powder my nose
Why are you so jealous when I flirt with the moon?
He's too old, you declare
you need someone younger
I don't think so
His experience is what I am after
and the sun's too
(though he may look bright, he's a bit wizened
under the chin)
So while I paint my fingernails with meteors dripping
liquid silver
you might stop to reconsider
Is there more to a woman that how she dresses?
I am airily painting my face blue
and decorating my toes with tiny ponds
a string of stars around my belly
but there is more to me
when you look past mere appearances

THE CURTAINS

This morning I tried to squeeze those white
curtains blue with my wishing eye
The white curtains fluttered in the breeze
morning sent in the window
My blue wish didn't die,
but drifted downstairs
A little boy cried for a blue balloon
lost in the wind.

HOW THIN

How thin my unyielding skin
The breezes you make in passing
swirl and flicker
Body makes no motion

How pale, the color of desire
Your strong handshake
in my limp hand
I cannot follow rapid strides

How distant, your fiery dream
Where you dance
I cannot go
Thought in chains

You chant, Begin again!
New seasons, unrelenting
Nothing stands still
My heart goes in circles

You force the warmth in
my unwilling cheek
I hold the perfect pearl
of no emotion

Passion curls inward still
You will pass
No need to feel or know or ache
A stone is safe

CIRCLE POEM

This poem is going in circles
First it found you there
Then it wound its way
into a clear glass of wine
then it giggled and fought
the utterly unbelievable concept of love
and wove an extremely complicated web
of deceit
It hid its head in piles of dust
It sang out of tune
It said I will love you later
when I am more aware of the effects of the phases of the moon
Large spaces must be traveled
Certain moments must be reasoned with
Regulations are in force, a long stream of
incomprehensible directions must be followed
You must prescribe to a necessary form
This poem isn't endless
It meets all criteria, knows its possibilities,
has no fears or qualms
It began, it ended
It found you there, quite simply,
the beginning
Making my poem move

TO SAY

Some things are so sought after
they button us down into silence
and from silence into ice

So there's a reason for flame
to start the cycle over
a repetition to be grateful for

Some think their lack of speech
a kind of purity, to make others
need them more

Holding love in cold crisis
forcing the other into heat
while they wait in deep freeze

Heedless of what you might say
I keep the flow moving
Seasons changing

No reason for it
Love, like that stupid blossom,
just keeps opening year after year after year

HEART

My large heart
never in a poem
pounds red ink
and keeps me up at night

My bloody heart
I never knew was there
swells inside my chest
demanding words

My fickle heart
split in two
hides her love
in bitter verse

My swollen heart
tells her lies
rides the surge
the angry storm

My selfish heart
pours through veins
a hidden pulse
What remains?

My leaking heart
gives herself away
all through the night
wails and keens

My innocent heart
scarcely beats
hiding inside
a thin shell of skin

My jealous heart
wants to claim all rights
Holds me in
Holds me tight

My perfect heart
knows herself
keeps quiet space
her dreams intact

My singing heart
knows no bounds
with metaphors
makes new songs

My faulty heart
her errors made
strives again
to make things right

My loving heart
so very blind
pumps poetry
for kindless souls

My hopeful heart
in endless rhyme
will beat for you
for little pay
will hold life still
and pain at bay
and never end
this poem

QUIET POEM

she was a sliver of moonlight
a tiny mountain in shadow
a basket of uneaten fruit

she rested in faint light
the rabbits stayed in their holes
no one came into her rooms

in distant hills tiny showers
could not find her
the summer stayed hot and full

the berries dropped slowly
deep in the forest
red stains did not touch her

a ripple of water
was all she could hear
she whispered to fish

the frogs were too loud
the birds too excited
she hid in the grass

she turned into thin blades
the green lit her eyes
as bright as shined glass

she rolled into nothing
as real as the day
her arms slender reeds

her mouth a slip of a stem
her heart barely heard

as alive as the wind

the dew was her belly
the pond weed her hair
she made the air still

she wove ribbons of silence
filling acres of space
the trees slowly bowed down

the deer led their young
to the edge of the stream
she flowed on and on and on

Alice Pero has been writing poetry for 17 years. She is a dancer, musician and teacher of creative writing. She has done many performances of poetry and dance in the New York City and Los Angeles areas. Dedicated to teaching creative writing, Alice has been a workshop leader for the New York City Ballet Education Department and The California Poets-in-the-Schools. This is her first book of poetry. She lives in La Crescenta, California with her dog, Josie.

Bruce Silton, illustrator, painter and designer, received his formal art education at the School of the Museum of Fine Arts in Boston. Over the past 31 years his paintings have been exhibited in America, England, France and Switzerland. In 1990 Bruce was awarded first place in drawing by the International Artists Guild.

For additional copies of *Thawed Stars* send $12.00 per book plus $3.00 for shipping and handling. California residents add 8.25% sales tax. Order through SunInk Publications, 37931 Palo Colorado Road, Carmel CA 93923 or from the author at P.O. Box 1089, La Cañada, CA 91012. pero@earthlink.net